FUN WITH COLORS!

Easy Painting Activities for Kids

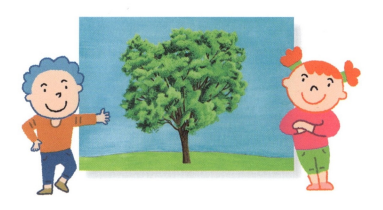

AZABU ATELIER

TUTTLE Publishing

Tokyo | Rutland, Vermont | Singapore

Getting Started

Do you enjoy painting?

Do the bright colors draw you in?

If you like to paint but feel you can't do it well or can't get the colors right, this is the book for you!

In this book, using only the art supplies commonly used in school, we'll introduce you to various methods for coloring. If you follow the instructions in this book, you'll be able to paint pictures that you'll be very happy with.

Painting and coloring may seem difficult at first, but as with any hobby, as you practice again and again, you will naturally get the hang of it.

Flip through this book, pick out projects you'd like to try coloring, and get started!

For the Adults

We run a children's art studio in Tokyo and spend time daily thinking about how children can freely enjoy creating art while also improving their skills.

Each child has their own creative individuality. In the studio, we ensure that our instruction about specific painting techniques and drawing methods is kept to a minimum, keeping a light hand on the tiller as we observe the children working freely while expressing their individuality.

Unlike in a studio, this book is designed to help children draw and paint independently, with the goal of standing in for an instructor who would help them when they're confused or don't understand something.

This book introduces the process of coloring pictures using basic art materials like watercolor paints and colored pencils in a way that children can easily understand. While there is no one right way to approach making art, we share our recommended techniques.

We hope this book encourages children to express their creativity through the joy of using color!

—Koichi Matsuda
Director of Azabu Atelier

CONTENTS

Getting Started ... 2
For the Adults ... 3
How to Use This Book ... 7

Chapter

Let's Get to Know the Tools for Coloring!

What Should I Do? —Tools Edition ... 10
Explore Familiar Art Supplies ... 12
Gather the Basic Tools ... 16
Choose the Right Paper to Use ... 22
Useful Items ... 24

Feature How to Arrange Your Workspace ... 26

Chapter 2: Discover the Secrets of Color!

What Should I Do? —Color Edition ... 28
Learn the Names of Colors ... 30
Understanding the Rules of Color ... 32
Creating New Colors ... 34
Adding Variation to Colors ... 36
Choosing Colors to Use ... 38

Feature The Way Colors Make Us Feel ... 40

Chapter 3: Learn the Ways of Coloring!

What Should I Do? —Drawing Edition ... 42
Sketching ... 44
Deciding on the Composition ... 46
Studying Your Subject ... 48
Learn the Order of Painting ... 50
Creating Soft Effects with Paint ... 52
Creating Gradients ... 56
Showing the Effects of Light and Shadow ... 60
Showing Texture ... 64

Feature Important Art Terms to Know ... 66

Chapter 4
Let's Make Colorful Art!

How to Paint an Apple ... 68
How to Paint Flowers ... 74
How to Paint the Sky ... 78
How to Paint a Tree ... 84
How to Paint Mountains ... 88
How to Paint the Sea ... 92
How to Draw Fireworks ... 96
How to Paint a Rabbit ... 100
How to Paint a Landscape ... 104
How to Paint a Car ... 110
Using Colored Pencils ... 114
How to Draw Flowers with Colored Pencils ... 116

Appendix A Color Blends ... 122
Appendix B Color Mixing Charts ... 124

Conclusion ... 126
Afterword ... 127

You can read this book in order, or start in any section you like—it's all good!

How to Use This Book

Before getting started, check out the themes of each chapter and the icons that appear throughout the book.

Chapters 1–3
Introduce types of art materials, knowledge about colors, and tips for coloring and painting.

Chapter 4
Explains how to draw and color various pictures such as The Sea, Animals and A Car.

① Difficulty
The more ⭐ symbols there are, the harder the activity is.

② Colors Used
Be sure you have the colors you need for the painting before starting.

③ Brush Icons
Round and flat brushes create different effects, so keep an eye out for these icons.

④ Notes, Tips and Cautions
Important information about painting and coloring appears in these boxes.

NOTE
Explains useful and important information to know.

TIP
Introduces ways to work that are helpful for expert coloring.

CAUTION
Info about tricky steps or possible problems to watch out for.

7

Characters Appearing in This Book

Professor Nekoda
A painting and coloring teacher. Known for his silly nature, he can appear suddenly beside children who are painting. He believes that the most important thing is to enjoy painting.

Makoto & Ai
Young students who love to paint. Excited about getting better at painting, they learn about painting and coloring from Professor Nekoda.

Chapter 1

Let's Get to Know the Tools for Coloring!

First, let's learn about the tools for coloring. Once you understand how all the tools work, you'll be able to color like an expert.

> **HELP!**

What Should I Do?

TOOLS EDITION!

Ai
Wow, your drawing is really good!
Um, is this round shape... is it an Asian pear?

Makoto
Thank you! But actually, it's an apple.

Ai
Oh, sorry! They look so similar; I got confused.

Makoto
Don't worry about it! Without color, it's difficult to tell one from the other.

Ai
Why don't you color it?

Chapter 1

Makoto: Well... there are so many tools—like paints and colored pencils—that I don't know which one to use!

Ai: That's true. The look of artwork changes depending on the tools used.

Makoto: I was thinking of using paints this time, but I'm worried I won't use them right.

Professor Nekoda: **But it's a snap if you learn how the tools work!**

Ai: Whoa! You scared us!

Makoto: Professor Nekoda, don't sneak up on us!

Professor Nekoda: I'm sorry. [Meow!] But since I'm here, I'd love for you to try using paints. Mixing colors and thinning them with water is so much fun!

Makoto: Do you think I can do it well?

Ai: Why don't we try together while learning from Professor Nekoda? Can I join in too, professor?

Professor Nekoda: Of course! Let's get started right away.

Let's Get to Know the Tools for Coloring!

WHAT KIND OF MATERIALS ARE THERE?

Explore Familiar Art Supplies

Tools for creating pictures are called *art supplies*. Each type of tool represents a different *medium*. Think about which art supplies to use for drawing or painting.

Difficulty Level

Coloring Media

Each medium has its own strengths and weaknesses. Check out the art supplies commonly used in schools!

Apply color freely!

Paints

Semi-transparent Watercolors

Paint that is partially see-through, an effect that becomes stronger when more water is added. It's easy to use and there are many ways to use it. Mix colors to create new ones.

Transparent Watercolors

Paint that gives a soft and gentle color. The first color painted can be seen through newer layers.

Acrylic Gouache ("Gwash")

Non-see-through paint that covers any color underneath. Once dried, you can layer colors on top.

12 Chapter 1

> Easy to use and handy!
>
> **Colored Pencils**

The color strength can be changed by changing how hard you press when coloring. You can also mix colors by layering them.

> Soft and smooth drawing
>
> **Crayons**

Allows you to draw thick, soft lines in bright colors. Crayons are recommended for covering large areas.

> Bright and clear colors
>
> **Markers**

There are water-based markers, where the lines can be blended with water, and oil-based markers, which are permanent. Depending on the type of marker, they can be used on surfaces other than paper.

Explore Familiar Art Supplies

Compare the Pictures

Let's compare apple pictures made using several different art supplies. Choose your materials based on the look you want to create.

Paints

By mixing the paints, you can create colors that match the ones you want to show.

 See page 68 for instructions on how to paint an apple!

Colored Pencils

These make bright colors that create a softer look. Lines and patterns are easy to make with colored pencils, which make detailed drawings possible.

In this book, we'll focus on paints, which are commonly used in schools!

Crayons

Soft lines create a warm look. The bright colors are eye-catching.

Markers

Oil-based alcohol markers are used here. They're great for drawing popular art like comics and manga.

THESE ARE MUST-HAVES!

Gather the Basic Tools

Collect the necessary tools for painting with watercolors. Also, let's take a look at how to use these tools.

Difficulty Level

Types of Brushes

The brushes used for watercolors basically fall into two types: *round brushes* and *flat brushes*. The different types of brushes have differently shaped tips, which affect the look of the lines.

Varying effects with one brush

Round Brush

A multi-use brush with a tip that comes to a point. By pressing harder, you can create thick lines, and by easing off, you can create thin lines.

16 Chapter 1

Easily paint with even thickness

Flat Brush

A brush with a flat, wide tip that makes it easy to paint lines of the same thickness. Unlike the round brush, it gives a neat and clean appearance to the edges of the lines.

NOTE

It's recommended to start with a set of three brushes: two round brushes and one flat brush. For the round brushes, choose one of medium thickness (size 8–10) and one that is thinner (size 2–6). For the flat brush, go for a thicker one (size 14–16).

The thickness of brushes is expressed in "sizes." The larger the number, the thicker the brush.

Let's Get to Know the Tools for Coloring! 17

Gather the Basic Tools

Using Different Brushes

When painting a picture, use different types of brushes to meet the needs of each area to be painted.
This will help you to apply color effectively.
Let's think about which brush to use for each part.

For Large Areas, Use a Flat Brush Boldly!
When applying paint to large areas like the sky, use a flat brush that can cover a lot of area in a single stroke.

CAUTION
Using a thin round brush to cover large areas will result in unevenness, and using a flat brush for small areas may cause you to paint outside the areas you want to color. Be sure to use the right brush!

For Small Areas, Use a Round Brush Carefully
For finer details, use a *fine* (thin) to medium round brush and take your time to paint carefully.

How to Wash Brushes

After you finish painting, clean your brushes so they're ready for the next use. Learn the correct way to wash brushes so they last a long time.

1 **Remove Paint from the Brush Tip**
Use a *brush washer* (like the one shown on page 20) to rinse off the paint from the brush tip with water.

2 **Remove Paint from the Brush Base**
Move the brush tip in a circular motion on your palm as if you are applying paint to release the paint soaked into the bristles at the base of the brush.

NOTE
If water alone doesn't remove the paint, adding some hand soap will help clean the brush completely.

3 **Dry the Brush with a Soft Cloth**
Use a soft cloth, such as a rag, to gently squeeze out most of the water from the brush tip. Once done, reshape the brush tip into a point and let it dry completely.

Gather the Basic Tools

How to Use a Brush Washer

A *brush washer* is a tool used to clean brushes. They come in various shapes, such as round bucket types or rectangular box types, but all have several compartments, each with a specific use.

1 First, use the larger compartment to wash off the paint from the brush.

2 Next, use the two smaller compartments to progressively rinse the brush clean.

3 One of the smaller compartments should be kept with clean water for diluting paint or creating gradients.

NOTE

PAPER CUPS WORK TOO!
If you don't have a brush washer, you can use paper or plastic cups instead. Prepare 3–4 cups and use them in the same way as the compartments in a brush washer.

How to Use a Palette

A *palette* is a tool used for holding and mixing paint. For watercolors that are thinned with water, a palette with some depth and separate compartments is recommended.

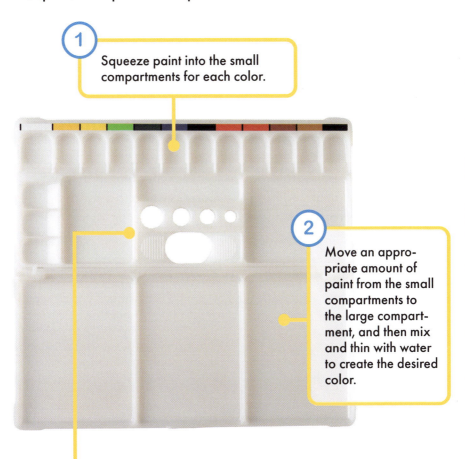

1 Squeeze paint into the small compartments for each color.

2 Move an appropriate amount of paint from the small compartments to the large compartment, and then mix and thin with water to create the desired color.

3 The large hole is for inserting your thumb to hold the palette easily.

The small holes are for gripping caps, making the tubes easy to open and close with one hand.

CHOOSE PAPER ACCORDING TO YOUR MATERIALS

Choose the Right Paper to Use

Be aware of the different types of paper and the coloring materials you'll use. Choose ones that will work well together.

Difficulty Level

Types of Paper

Choosing the right paper for your media can help you create better art. Among the many types of paper available, we introduce papers that are suitable for the media discussed on pages 12–13.

Recommended for practice

Drawing Paper | Recommended materials: Paints, Crayons

Often used for drawing and crafts. Available at stationery shops and even at dollar stores. Start with this paper to get used to using paints.

CAUTION

If too much water is applied, the paper can warp or disintegrate, leaving fiber clumps. Use watercolor paper or thicker drawing paper for better results.

Chapter 1

> Good for water-based techniques

Watercolor Paper

Recommended materials: Paints (semi-transparent watercolor, transparent watercolor)

Perfect for techniques that use a lot of water, like blending and blurring. The textured surface makes it easy to apply color evenly.

CAUTION

If you use less water with the paint, you won't be able to get the full benefit of the watercolor paper. For acrylic gouache, use drawing paper instead.

> Ideal for detailed work

Kent Paper

Recommended materials: Colored Pencils, Markers

The smooth surface of Kent paper allows for fine, detailed lines. It's also good for even color coverage.

CAUTION

Because the surface is not very "thirsty," using paint with a lot of water—like transparent watercolors—can create streaks. When painting, use less water.

Let's Get to Know the Tools for Coloring!

EXPAND YOUR RANGE OF EXPRESSION

Useful Items

Here are some handy tools that make painting and drawing even more enjoyable.

Difficulty Level

Useful Tools Around You

While you can paint or draw with just the necessary tools, using some extra tools can create new effects and make your artwork look even better.

Create the perfect color

Dropper

A tool for adding water drop by drop, allowing you to adjust colors exactly as you want. It can also be used to mix colors by taking up watered-down paint and adding it to other colors.

Dropping paint directly onto the paper with a dropper might also create interesting effects!

> Simply stick it on

Masking Tape

By sticking on masking tape and then painting over it, you can leave white areas and sharp edges on the paper after you peel it off. Be careful not to tear the paper when removing the tape.

Stick on the masking tape in a rectangular shape before painting.

Once you finish painting, peel off the masking tape to reveal the clean edges.

> Use it like a stamp

Kneaded Eraser

Lighten pencil lines drawn as a base sketch so that the lines don't stand out boldly when you paint over them with transparent paint. It doesn't erase as completely as a regular eraser, making it easy to lighten the marks without completely removing the lines.

GATHER THE BASIC TOOLS

[How to Arrange Your Workspace]

Place the tools on the desk where they are within easy reach. Also, be careful not to stain the desk or floor.

• Note: The photo shows the setup for right-handed people. If you're left-handed, reverse all the tool placements.

Palette

Paints

Newspaper — Because paint might overflow or splash off the drawing paper, always lay down a layer of newspaper underneath.

Drawing Paper

Brushes • Brush Washer • Cloth — Place all three together on your drawing-hand side. The cloth is used to dry the brush.

Discover the Secrets of Color!

There are many ways to use colors together. To make the most of each color's beauty in your paintings and drawings, it's important to understand the way colors work together.

HELP!

What Should I Do?

COLOR EDITION

Ai
> Now that we know how to use the tools, let's start painting!

Professor Nekoda
> Wait a moment! There's something important to learn before using the paints. [Meow!]

Ai
> Something important?

Professor Nekoda
> It's all about "colors!"

Makoto
> Colors? You mean like red and orange? I know about those...

Professor Nekoda
> Hehe... But do you know how orange is made?

Makoto
> What? Isn't orange just... orange!?

Professor Nekoda
> Earlier, I mentioned that one of the fun parts about using paints is mixing colors and thinning them with water... Makoto, try mixing red and yellow paints.

Makoto: Okay. ...Ah, it changed to an orange color!

Ai: Amazing! It's like magic.

Professor Nekoda: Just like this, colors change when you mix them. By combining paints from the primary colors—red, blue and yellow—you can create new colors!

Ai: So, even though we only have 12 colors of paint in our set, we can create and use even more colors!

Makoto: What about thinning them in water?

Professor Nekoda: Oh, you're getting curious, aren't you? Want to learn more about colors?

Ai & Makoto: We want to know more!

Professor Nekoda: That's the right outlook! Let's start learning about colors right away!

Discover the Secrets of Color! 29

HOW MANY COLORS DO YOU KNOW?

Learn the Names of Colors

Each color has a name.
Let's look at the paint colors used in this book.

Difficulty Level ★☆☆

Twelve Basic Colors

Paint sets generally contain the most frequently used colors.
Let's learn the colors in the basic 12-color set.

• Note: Color types and names vary depending on the maker. Here, we'll use the 12-color set from "Pentel F Watercolor" as an example.

In addition to the basic 12 colors, various other colors of paint are available. Purple is highly recommended as it is frequently used for shading. Enjoy experimenting with gold and silver to add a sparkling look to your art!

In Chapter 4, we'll use these 12 colors to paint and draw pictures!

Discover the Secrets of Color! 31

HOW COLORS ARE MIXED!

Understanding the Rules of Color

When mixing colors, there are specific relationships to understand.

Difficulty Level

The Way Color Blending Works

Let's learn the ideas behind how colors are mixed. This information will be useful when mixing colors or selecting them while using paints.

Primary Colors

By mixing the three primary colors of paint—red, blue and yellow—you can create brown. By changing the amount of these three colors or using only two, you can make many different colors.

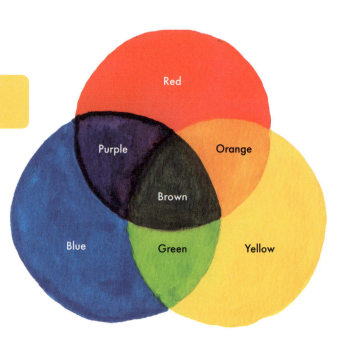

Chapter 2

Color Wheel

Colors like red, blue, and purple are referred to as *hues*. A *color wheel* is a circular arrangement of hues that are related to each other.

By looking at the color wheel, you can easily see the relationships between colors! Check out page 38 for more details.

Discover the Secrets of Color!

MIXING PAINTS

Creating New Colors

Mixing two or more paints to create a different color is called *color mixing*.

The Rules of Color Mixing

When creating colors through color mixing, there are specific "recipes" to follow. Additionally, the more colors you use, the more varied the shades will become.

Two-Color Mixing

A brown color made by mixing orange and purple. Compared to three-color mixing, the hue is more *vivid* (bright and bold) and distinct.

Three-Color Mixing

A brown color made by mixing red, blue and yellow. This results in a softer color compared to two-color mixing.

 The vividness of a color is called *saturation*. Controlling saturation can be challenging, so it's best to start with two-color mixing!

Tips for Color Mixing

Color mixing is a basic skill in painting, but creating the right color can be hard even for full-time artists. Remember these instructions and practice mixing to create the colors you want.

Use Clean Water and Brushes

If the water used to dissolve the paints is dirty or the brush tip is dirty, it will affect the hue.

Make More Than You Need

By creating a bit more paint than you think you'll need, you can prevent running out while painting.

Test on a Separate Paper

When mixing a second batch to match a color that you've run out of, apply the new mixture onto a separate paper first to ensure there is no difference in color.

Discover the Secrets of Color! 35

DIFFERENT SHADES OF THE SAME HUE!

Adding Variation to Colors

You can change the shades of colors by mixing in black or white paint, or by adding water.

Difficulty Level ★★★

Mixing Black and White

The brightness of a color is called its *value*. By mixing black or white paint with other colors, you can change the value of those colors.

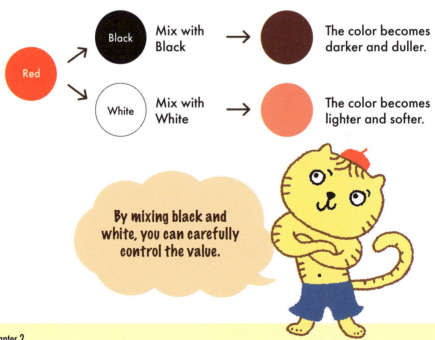

Red → Black → Mix with Black → The color becomes darker and duller.

Red → White → Mix with White → The color becomes lighter and softer.

By mixing black and white, you can carefully control the value.

Mixing with Water

Adding water makes the paint appear thinner and more transparent. You can adjust the amount of water to create *gradients* (gradual changes in color—see pages 56–59) or layer colors to let the underlying colors show through.

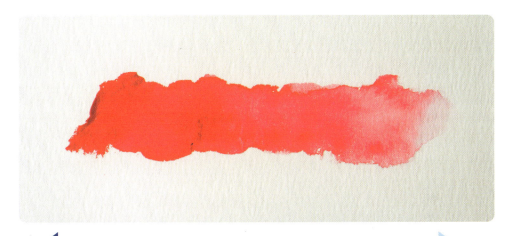

← Less Water   Amount of Water   More Water →

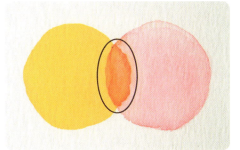

Layering Thick Paint

When you layer thick paint with less water on top of dried paint, the underlying color will not show through.

Layering Thin Paint

When you layer thin paint with more water, the underlying paint color will show through, and the overlapping area will appear as a different color.

Discover the Secrets of Color!

CHOOSING COLORS TO PAINT

Choosing Colors to Use

Find colors that go well together from the endless number of colors available.

Difficulty Level ★★★

Relationships Between Colors

By looking at the color wheel on page 33, you can recognize the combinations of related colors. Let's learn about *analogous colors*, which are similar colors next to each other on a color wheel, and *complementary colors*, which are opposite each other on the wheel.

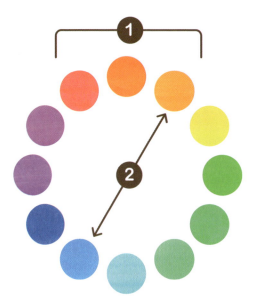

 Analogous Colors

Combinations of similar colors that are next to each other on the wheel. These tend to look like they belong together.

 Complementary Colors

Combinations of colors that are opposite each other on the wheel. These combinations create a lively and attention-grabbing look.

Tips for Choosing Colors

There are rules for combining colors in a pleasing way. By following these rules, your painting will look beautiful and well put together.

These three colors are analogous colors, but they don't seem to belong together.

Changing the color on the right to a lighter shade of the same hue creates a sense of unity.

Matching the brightness (value) and vividness (saturation) of the colors is key!

1 Matching Color Value

Bright ↕ Dark

2 Matching Color Saturation

Vivid ↕ Dull

Discover the Secrets of Color!

The Way Colors Make Us Feel

Each color suggests a certain feeling in people's minds.

For example, should the word "caution" be written in red or blue? Remembering these associations can be useful when creating posters or signs.

Warm Colors (Warm Image)
- **Red** — A color that feels hot and energetic. It is also used to indicate danger or caution.
- **Orange** — Conveys a fun and lively sense. It has a healthy image.
- **Yellow** — Bright and hopeful. When combined with black, it implies caution.

Neutral Color
- **Green** — Calm and soothing. It is the color of nature, such as grass and leaves.

Cool Colors (Cool Image)
- **Blue** — Cool and quiet. It can also suggest a lonely feeling, like someone crying.
- **Navy Blue** — A dignified color. Often used in uniforms and business suits.
- **Purple** — Mysterious and intriguing. It is a sophisticated color—the color of royalty.

Neutral Color
- **Pink** — A playful color that makes one's heart flutter. It also suggests kindness and sweetness.

Neutral colors can be considered as both warm and cool colors.

Learn the Ways of Coloring!

Discover techniques and know-how that will help you make your artwork look better and more expertly made. Some of these might be tricky, so try to using them little by little.

HELP!

What Should I Do?

DRAWING EDITION

Ai

> Wow, there's so much depth to colors!

Professor Nekoda

> Right? If you use colors skillfully, your drawings will look even more beautiful!

Makoto

> Once we've chosen the colors, it's finally time to color. I wonder if I can do it well.

Ai

> When I try to color small details, I end up going outside the lines or the colors get muddy....

Professor Nekoda

> That can happen to anyone, Ai.

Makoto

> I want to make it look great, but it never turns out the way I want....

Ai

> Professor Nekoda, is there a way to color neatly?

Professor Nekoda

> Alright. For you two who have worked hard so far, I'll teach you "Professor Nekoda's method" to make your drawings look great with coloring!

Ai Makoto

Yay!

Professor Nekoda

Some of the tips I'm about to share are difficult, so you might not get them right away. But with practice, you'll definitely improve!

Ai

Practice.... That's right, even if I mess up, I can just try again!

Makoto

It's unusual to be good at something right from the start.

Professor Nekoda

Exactly. As you complete each piece, you'll find yourself getting better and better without even realizing it.

Makoto

I feel like drawing and coloring all sorts of things now!

Ai

Me too!

Professor Nekoda

You're really motivated! I'll be excited to teach you too!

Ai Makoto

Thanks, Professor! Please begin!

Learn the Ways of Coloring! 43

START BY BUILDING A FOUNDATION

Sketching

Before starting to add color, let's create the basic sketch that will form the basis of your painting.

Difficulty Level

How to Draw a Basic Sketch

While it's fun to start adding color directly and freely, creating a basic *preliminary sketch* to decide what and how to color or paint can help you work more effectively later on.

It is recommended to use 2B or HB pencils.

Use a pencil to draw the shapes of objects. Decide on the arrangement (*composition*—see page 46) at the same time as you draw the preliminary sketch.

If the lines of the sketch seem too dark, use a kneaded eraser to lightly dab at the lines to lighten them.

Preliminary Sketch Techniques

You can use materials other than pencils to draw the preliminary sketch. The look of the drawing will change depending on the material used. Choose according to the type of drawing or object you want to create.

Drawing with a Marker
This creates clear, comic book or manga-like outlines. Be sure to use oil-based markers if you'll be using watercolor paints, as water-based marker lines will smear when wet.

Drawing with Crayons
This creates soft, gentle lines. Because the crayon wax holds up against watercolor paint, you can paint over it as well.

By combining various materials, you might discover new ways to express yourself!

SHAPE THE VIEWER'S IMPRESSIONS

Deciding on the Composition

The placement of each element on the paper is called *composition*.

Difficulty Level

Showing Depth

Showing different distances for objects placed within a painting or drawing creates the look of depth. Include these three aspects in your compositions: *foreground*, *middle ground*, and *background*.

② Middle Ground
Objects in the middle. They connect the foreground and the background.

③ Background
Objects farthest away. This aspect is important for adding depth to the composition.

① Foreground
Objects in the front. Things in the foreground should appear largest.

Tips for Composition

Along with the three distances, here are some key points to consider when deciding on your composition. By creatively arranging your composition, you can call attention to what you want to highlight.

Change the Arrangement
The position of objects on the paper can change the feeling of the composition. For example, shifting an object slightly to the left or right can create a sense of open space.

Change the Size (*Scale*)
Depicting foreground objects so large that they extend off the edge can add depth. In this case, position what you want to highlight (the building) in the middle ground.

Change the Angle of View (*Perspective*)
Besides viewing from a standing position at eye level, consider looking down from above (*bird's eye view*) or looking up from below (*worm's eye view*). This is recommended for showing elevation or for dramatic effect.

COLOR AND SHAPE ARE KEY

Studying Your Subject

Before starting a preliminary sketch or adding color, take time to carefully look at (*observe*) the subject you plan to draw or paint.

Difficulty Level

Notes About Observation

When drawing or painting something, focus on its color and shape. These things are very important for clearly showing what the object is to the viewer.

Color

Look for not only the main color of the object, but also the colors that appear due to the object's surface type, and "hidden" colors that you might not usually notice.

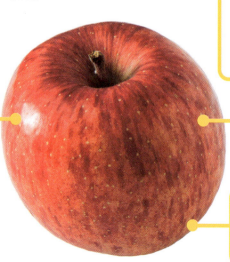

The natural red of the object (an apple). There are various shades of red, including pinkish-red and reddish-orange.

The color of the white light reflecting off the shiny object. For more on light, check page 60.

Discover the yellow hidden within the red.

48 Chapter 3

| Shape | Some objects have a standard shape. Drawing or painting these shapes accurately makes it easier for viewers to recognize the object. |

The apple from earlier is roughly circular! However, it's not a perfect circle— the shape has dips and bumps, and there's a stem.

Complex Shapes
For objects with complex shapes, it is easier to think of them as combinations of several simple shapes rather than a single complicated form.

Learn the Ways of Coloring!

FOR BEAUTIFUL COLORS

Learn the Order of Painting

By following the correct order when applying paint, you can paint without the colors becoming muddy.

Difficulty Level

Basic Painting Order

When thinking about the order, concentrate on the concepts of color value and area size. Start with light colors and large areas. After painting a layer, let it dry well before applying the next color.

Color — Begin with light colors, colors close to white, or colors thinned with a lot of water, and then move on to darker and more saturated colors. By following this order, the paint is less likely to appear muddy.

1. .... The lightest color: White
2. .... Bright colors and colors close to white, such as yellow, pink and sky blue
3. .... Primary colors like red, blue and green
4. .... Dark and saturated colors like brown and navy blue
5. .... The darkest color: Black

Chapter 3

| Area | After color, the next important thing is the size of the area to be painted. Start with large areas and finish with the smaller details.

Paint large areas—like the background—first
When painting large areas, use a wide flat brush or a *hake* brush to avoid unevenness and create a relatively streak-free appearance.

Paint narrow areas and small details
Use a round brush for small areas and fine details, like eyes. Paint colors thinned with water first.

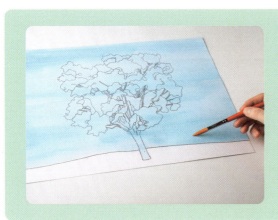

Paint Without Worrying About the Outline
If you plan to paint large areas with watered-down colors and small areas or fine details with darker or more *opaque* (non-see-through) colors, it's okay to first cover the entire sketch with the thinned colors. Once dry, apply the darker or more opaque colors!

Learn the Ways of Coloring! 51

YOU'LL WANT TO TRY USING THIS!

Creating Soft Effects with Paint

By using water and tools in addition to painting with brushes, you can create new effects.

Difficulty Level ★★

Common Techniques

Here are some common techniques like *blurring* and *bleeding*, which occur when water and paint mix on the paper, *blotting*, where you intentionally remove applied paint, and *spattering*, where you flick paint, creating tiny splashes.

Soft color tones

Blurring

This technique involves gently spreading the applied paint with a wet brush to create a gradient.

Apply paint to the paper. Leave a little distance between the edge of the painted area and the sketch line.

Before the paint dries, use a clean, wet brush to blend and spread the edges of the paint.

> Enjoy the freedom
>
> **Bleeding**

This technique involves slowly spreading the paint with water. It's a little difficult because it can't be strictly controlled.

Use a brush to apply water to the paper. Apply water only where necessary to prevent the paint from spreading too much.

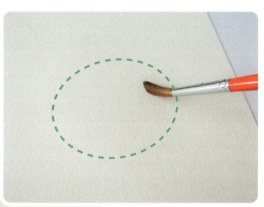

Layer on diluted paint before the water dries.

How to Use Blurring and Bleeding for Different Effects
Use blurring to naturally color shadows, and bleeding to create soft, cloudy filled-in areas wherever needed!

Blurring

Learn the Ways of Coloring! 53

Creating Soft Effects with Paint

For see-through color

Blotting

By dabbing some paint away with a tissue before it dries, you can create patterns or add variation to the color.

This painting has had the cloud parts blotted with tissue. The transparent look and the fluffy edges of the clouds create a natural look.

First, apply paint to the paper. To prevent it from drying too quickly, use a slightly more watered-down mixture.

Shape a tissue into a little bundle, and then use it to gently blot the paint with a tapping motion.

> Scrub and spatter
>
> **Spattering**

This technique uses a spatter screen and a brush to flick speckles of paint.

> Because the paint will spatter, be sure to cover the surrounding area with newspaper to prevent overspray!

This painting mimics the look of falling snow through spattering. This technique is also recommended for depicting twinkling night skies or splashing water.

Gently load up slightly water-thinned paint on the screen using a brush. The paint should be somewhat thick for best results.

Scrub the mesh with an old toothbrush to flick the paint. The farther the screen is from the paper, the more spread out the paint spatter will be.

Learn the Ways of Coloring!

ENJOYING COLOR VARIATION

Creating Gradients

A *gradient* is a painting technique that uses color blending to gradually change the strength of the paint.

Difficulty Level

Single-Color Gradients

Gradients can make a painting look much more polished. When creating a gradient with just one color, adjust the amount of water to vary the strength of the paint.

Creating gradients from dark to light is done by *blending*.

A painting of the sky done with a gradient. The smooth gradient gives the feeling of a large space like the real sky, rather than painting everything flatly with the same concentration of color.

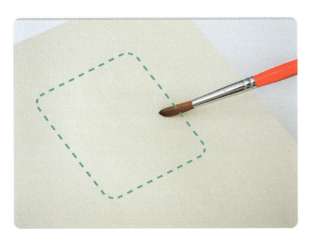

Apply water to the paper
Use a brush to apply water to the area where you want the gradient to appear.

Paint from the top
Start painting from the side where you want the color to be darkest. Fully load the brush with paint and move it across the paper in a zigzag motion.

To Avoid Unevenness
Once you start painting, continue to the end without stopping to prevent unevenness. Paint quickly before the water you applied to the paper dries!

Learn the Ways of Coloring! 57

Creating Gradients

Two-Color Gradients

Using two colors of paint creates new colors within the gradient as they mix. Find your favorite color combinations.

Creating the look of an ice cream float with a gradient of yellow and green creates a more convincing look than using just green.

CAUTION

For color combinations, refer to the "analogous colors" introduced on page 38 for beautiful gradients. Be cautious with "complementary colors" as mixing them can cause muddiness.

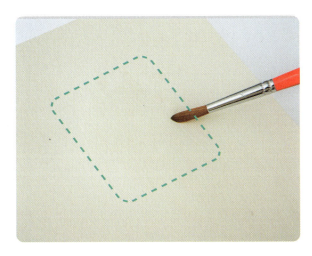

Use a brush to apply water
As with the way to create a single-color gradient, use a brush to apply water to the paper.

Paint from both sides
Apply the first color up to about the middle of the gradient. Start applying the second color from the opposite side, stopping before it overlaps with the first color.

Blend the middle
Before the paint dries, blend the middle of the gradient with a brush.

Learn the Ways of Coloring! 59

MAKING A PAINTING IMPRESSIVE

Showing the Effects of Light and Shadow

Learn the basics of how light and shadow work to use them into your painting.

Difficulty Level

The Way Light and Shadow Work

Having realistic light and shadow shown in a painting instantly makes it look more impressive. The key is to consider the source of the light. Once you understand where the light is coming from and where the shadows form, you can draw and paint freely.

Objects cast shadows
Shadows are formed when light from a light source is blocked by people or objects.

Light sources produce... light!
Things that project light, such as the sun or light bulbs, are called *light sources*.

The direction that shadows fall changes with the direction of light
Shadows always form on the opposite side of the direction of the light source. If the light is coming from the right, the shadow will be on the left side of the object.

The shape changes depending on the object
A round ball creates a round or oval shadow, while people and animals create shadows that match their shapes.

Highlights
When light bounces off the surface of an object directly to the viewer's eye, it creates what is called a *highlight*. Areas where highlights occur appear white because the object is reflecting the light strongly.

Showing the Effects of Light and Shadow

Showing Light and Shadow in a Painting

Once you understand how light and shadow work, show it in your paintings. First, figure out the direction the light is traveling, then draw or paint shadows and reflections with color. If it's tough to decide how to show the light reflected onto an object from its surroundings (option ③, below), at least show options ① and ②.

Practice showing the way light and shadows affect various shapes and objects! Depending on the object, changing the color of the shadows and reflections can also look beautiful.

62 Chapter 3

Creating highlights with white

To represent highlights as explained on page 61, either leave the reflecting areas unpainted or overlay with white paint in certain parts for a clean effect.

Using purple or navy blue for shadows is also recommended

For shadows, in addition to black and gray, you can use colors like purple and navy blue. These colors make the overall painting appear brighter than using black.

Creating midtones with gradients

If you want to include areas of light and shadow side by side, use gradients. Start painting from the shadow areas and gradually lighten as you move toward the lighter areas.

Learn the Ways of Coloring!

YOU CAN PAINT THINGS REALISTICALLY

Showing Texture

Here are ways to show the look and feel of objects in a painting.

Difficulty Level ★★☆

The Texture of Objects

The look and feel of objects, such as smooth, shiny or fluffy, are called *texture*. Let's discuss the key points for showing texture in a painting.

Smooth surface

Tomato

By making the areas where light reflects and appears white, you can create a shiny, slick look. Observe carefully to understand the shape of the light areas.

Be sure to observe the object carefully!

It's easier to add light spots by painting the entire area and letting it dry before adding the white areas.

64 Chapter 3

Glossy finish

Clip

The part where light hits the edge of metal and appears white is called the *highlight*. Carefully paint or draw the highlights exactly as they appear to depict glossy objects.

Clearly create contrasting areas of shadow and light.

Soft and fluffy feel

Towel

To show the fluffiness of towels and stuffed animals, or the furry feel of animal hair, use fine brush strokes.

Imagine the flow of the threads or hair while drawing or painting.

Important Art Terms to Know

When discussing paintings and drawings, specialized words are often used. Here are explanations of some commonly used terms.

Motif
The "subject" of the drawing or painting. It also refers to the inspiration for the artwork. It could also be called the "theme."

Depth
The sense of three-dimensionality created by the arrangement of objects, use of colors, and light and shadow in a painting. It creates the sense of space.

Painterly
A term that describes the look of a painting with objects shown mainly through areas of color, brushstrokes and textures rather than with defining outlines.

Tone
The overall value and saturation of colors. By carefully varying the tone throughout your paintings, you can create the look of three-dimensionality.

Let's Make Colorful Art!

In this chapter, we provide step-by-step explanations to show you how to draw and paint different subjects. Follow along with the photos and text as you work.

Difficulty Level

How to Paint an Apple

Apples are a perfect motif for practicing with paints.
Try painting while keeping in mind how to use mixed colors,
show the surface's gloss, and portray light and shadow.

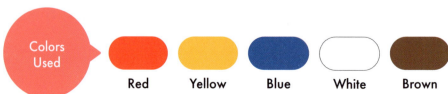

Colors Used — Red, Yellow, Blue, White, Brown

Sketch the Outlines

Check pages 62-63 for tips on making shadows and highlights!

1 **Draw an Apple**
Draw the apple with a pencil. First, draw the outline of the apple, then decide on the position of the shadows and highlights.

Layer on the Red

It's okay to fill in the shadows and highlights too.

2 **Paint the Entire Apple**
Paint the entire apple with a thin layer of red mixed with plenty of water.

3 **Apply More Layers of Red**
Apply another layer of red mixed with less water than in step 2. Leave out the large highlighted areas.

Color Used — Red

Color Used — Red

Let's Make Colorful Art!

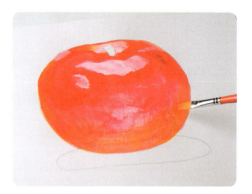

You'll use a lot of purple in later steps, so make extra!

④ Layer on Yellow
Using yellow mixed with water, paint the parts of the apple that have turned yellow from the left to the bottom side.

Color Used: Yellow

⑤ Layer on Purple
Mix red and blue to make purple. Dilute some purple with more water, and apply it to the darker areas of the apple.

Colors Used: Red + Blue

⑥ Make It Even Darker
Using purple mixed with less water than in step 5, layer the color to make it even darker.

Color Used: ⑤ Purple

NOTE

Compare your progress to the first layer of color. Gradually layering colors to deepen the shade will help you paint well.

Chapter 4

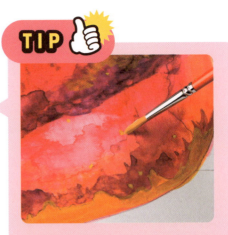

(7) Paint the Pattern
Using yellow mixed with a small amount of water, paint the details on the apple. Paint the bottom side of the apple and near the stem.

TIP — For dot patterns, it's easier to paint using the tip of a fine round brush!

Color Used: Yellow

Use diluted paint when you add speckles to the glossy areas to strengthen the sense of realism.

(8) Paint the Highlights
Paint the shiny, glossy parts where the light is hitting using white mixed with water.

Color Used: White

Let's Make Colorful Art!

Paint the Stem

Mix yellow with some of the purple from step ⑤ and paint the entire stem. Similarly, mix brown with some purple from step ⑤ and layer the stem with it.

  +
Purple   Yellow

⑤ + Brown
Purple   Brown

⑩ Paint the Shadow
Paint the shadow under the apple with the purple from step ⑤ to complete it.

If you paint dark blue just below the apple, you can add three-dimensionality to the painting.

 ⑤
Purple

72   Chapter 4

Fruit Examples

Pineapple

The spiky pineapple is one of the more difficult fruits to paint. Make it with jagged outlines.

Mixed Fruit

Oranges and grapes may seem to be similar in color, but they actually have different values and saturations.

Let's Make Colorful Art!

How to Paint Flowers

Even with just a single color, you can show texture by layering different values and saturations (page 39). Leaves have veins, so observe them closely and paint them in detail.

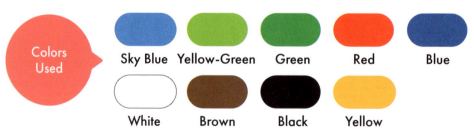

Sketch the Outlines

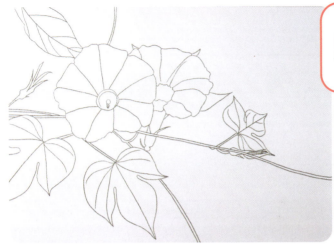

When drawing petals, consider their shape and overlap for a beautiful result.

Draw the Flowers and Leaves
Use a pencil to draw the flowers and leaves. Include the stems and buds as well.

Paint the Flowers and Leaves

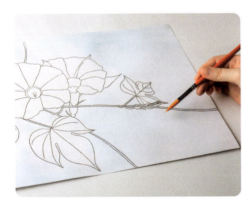

② Paint the Background

Use sky blue diluted with plenty of water to paint the background.

Color Used Sky Blue

③ Paint the Leaves

Mix yellow-green and green, dilute with water, and paint the leaves, stems and buds.

Colors Used  Yellow-Green Green

Let's Make Colorful Art! 75

When painting leaves, move the brush along the veins of the leaves!

④ Paint the Flowers

Mix red, blue and white to create a light purple, and dilute with water. Leave the white part in the center of the flowers unpainted.

Colors Used: Red + Blue + White

⑤ Layer the Leaves

Mix a little black with green. Layer this mixture over the leaves, stems and buds.

Colors Used: Green + Black

⑥ Paint the Shadows on the Leaves

Mix brown and yellow with the green from step ⑤, and dilute with water. Paint the shadows of the leaves and buds, and layer it on the stems.

Colors Used: Green ⑤ + Brown + Yellow

⑦ Layer the Flowers (Part 1)

Mix red and blue to create purple, and layer it to deepen the overall color of the petals.

Colors Used: Red + Blue

8) Layer the Flowers (Part 2)

Use light pink diluted with water to layer only the parts of the petals that are overlapping and creating shadows.

Color Used Pink

9) Paint the Center of the Flowers

Use green diluted with plenty of water to lightly paint the center of the flowers, and then layer white diluted with water on top.

Colors Used Green White

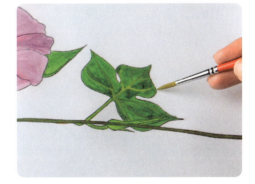

10) Paint the Shadows of the Flowers

Use a slightly darker purple than in step ⑦ to layer the shadows of the petals and the darker areas.

Color Used Purple

11) Paint the Leaf Veins

Detail the leaf veins with yellow-green diluted with water to complete the painting.

Color Used Yellow-Green

Let's Make Colorful Art!

Difficulty Level

How to Paint the Sky

The sky, often filled with solid blue or light blue, looks more sophisticated when you add gradients, accent colors and clouds. Try not only mixing colors on the palette before painting but also blending the painted colors directly on the paper.

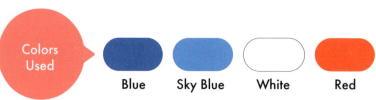

Colors Used — Blue, Sky Blue, White, Red

Sketch the Outlines

Draw the Clouds
Use a pencil to outline the clouds. Varying the shapes and sizes creates a natural look.

Paint the Sky

> Using a thick, flat brush or a *hake* brush makes it easier!

② **Paint the Sky**

Dilute blue and sky blue with water, and paint the entire sky. Paint so that the color lightens toward the bottom.

③ **Darken the Sky Color**

Dilute blue with water and layer it over the entire sky, avoiding the clouds.

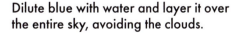
Color Used — Blue

Colors Used

Blue + Sky Blue

Let's Make Colorful Art! 79

NOTE

Intentionally creating unevenness gives the clouds texture and a see-through look!

④ Paint the Clouds (Part 1)

Paint the clouds with white diluted with plenty of water. Dab the brush lightly to spread the paint.

Color Used: 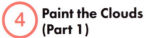 White

The white will blend if applied before the paint dries.

⑤ Paint the Clouds (Part 2)

Blend the edges of the clouds with white on the paper. Add small, ragged clouds.

Color Used: White

6 Add Shadows to the Clouds

Mix blue and white, dilute with water, and paint the shadowed parts of the clouds.

Colors Used:  Blue White

7 Cover the Sketch Lines

Use thick white paint with minimal water to cover the sketch lines.

Color Used: White

8 Layer More White

Blend more white into the blue from step ⑥, and apply thicker layers of white.

Color Used:  White

TIP

To create the fluffy texture of clouds, move the brush in circular motions while painting.

Let's Make Colorful Art!   81

Paint the upper side darker and the lower side slightly lighter for a nice effect.

⑨ Darken the Entire Sky

Mix a little red with blue to create blue-purple. Layer this color over the entire sky to darken it.

Colors Used: Blue + Red

⑩ Darken the Cloud Shadows

Add white to the blue-purple from step ⑨, dilute with water, and layer it over the overlapping parts of the clouds to complete the shadows.

Colors Used: Purple ⑨ + White

Sky Example

Mixing yellow instead of blue creates a sky that looks as if it's being warmed by the sunlight.

Sky and Mountains

Here is a powerful painting showing mountains towering higher than the clouds. The hot air balloon, mountains and sky form a variety of motifs within a single painting.

Adjust the cloud colors to reflect the sky color.

Let's Make Colorful Art!

Difficulty Level

How to Paint a Tree

Think big and paint the spread of the branches with boldness. Form the leaves not by depicting each one, but by using brush strokes to suggest clumps. Use different colors for the parts in sunlight and the parts in the shadows (pages 62–63).

Colors Used: Sky Blue, Yellow-Green, Brown, Green

Sketch the Outlines

Define the areas where the leaves gather in clumps and draw them roughly.

Draw the Tree
Draw the tree with a pencil. After drawing the trunk, draw the branches and leaves while thinking about the overall balance.

Paint the Tree

It's okay to fill in the tree with sky blue too!

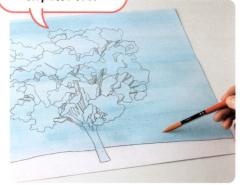

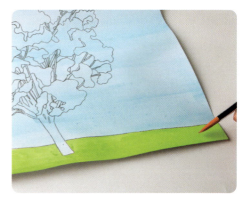

② Paint the Sky

Use diluted sky blue to paint the sky.

Color Used — Sky Blue

③ Paint the Ground

Use diluted yellow-green to paint the ground.

Color Used — Yellow-Green

Let's Make Colorful Art! 85

4. Paint the Leaves

Dilute the yellow-green from step ③ with water and paint the leaves. After painting inside the lines, paint slightly beyond the edges, into the gaps.

Color Used — ③ Yellow-Green

5. Paint the Trunk and Branches

Mix a little yellow-green with brown, dilute with water, and paint the trunk and branches.

Colors Used — Brown + Yellow-Green

Dab the paint lightly with the brush tip.

6. Paint the Shadows of the Leaves

Mix yellow-green and green, dilute with water, and paint the shadowed parts of the leaves.

Colors Used — Yellow-Green + Green

7. Blend the Shadows

Mix yellow-green with the green from step ⑥ and blend the boundary between the yellow-green from step ③ and the green from step ⑥.

Colors Used — ⑥ Yellow-Green + ③ Green

8 Paint the Trunk Details

Use brown diluted with less water than in step ⑤ to make the grooves in the bark on the trunk.

Color Used
Brown

9 Darken the Shadows of the Tree

Dilute green with water and add more layers to the darker parts of the leaf shadows.

Color Used
 Green

> Blend these shadows with the ones from step ⑦, just as in step ⑨.

10 Paint the Sunlit Parts

Use diluted yellow-green to paint the parts of the leaves where light is hitting.

Color Used
 Yellow-Green

11 Add More Shadows

Dilute green with water and add more layers to the leaf shadows to complete the painting.

Color Used
 Green

Let's Make Colorful Art!

Difficulty Level

How to Paint Mountains

Create a color gradient to show the sense of depth with overlapping mountains. Showing the details of objects in the foreground makes the painting look even better.

Colors Used

Sky Blue

Blue

Black

Sketch the Outlines

Instead of drawing details like tree branches, try drawing just the outlines.

① Draw the Trees and Mountains

Start by drawing the trees in the foreground, then draw seven mountain ridges in the background. Draw the mountains with jagged lines.

Paint the Sky and Mountains

② Paint the Sky

Apply a thin layer of water to the sky area. Then, layer sky blue diluted with water over it.

③ Paint the Distant Mountains

Add a little blue to the sky blue from step ② to make it slightly darker than the sky, and use this color to paint the most distant mountain ridge.

Color Used — Sky Blue

Colors Used — Sky Blue ➕ Blue

Let's Make Colorful Art! 89

> Add black paint gradually to avoid over-mixing.

④ Paint the Second Mountain Ridge

As in step ③, mix a bit more blue with sky blue to paint the second mountain ridge from the back.

Colors Used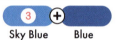
Sky Blue + Blue

⑤ Paint the Third Mountain Ridge

Mix a little black with blue to paint the third mountain ridge from the back.

Colors Used
Blue + Black

⑥ Paint the Fourth Mountain Ridge

Use blue diluted with water to paint the fourth mountain ridge from the back.

Color Used
Blue

⑦ Paint the Fifth Mountain Ridge

Mix a bit more black with blue than in step ⑤. Use this color to paint the fifth mountain ridge from the back.

Colors Used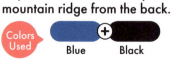
Blue + Black

You can see the gradient from the distant mountains!

⑧ Paint the Sixth Mountain Ridge

Mix more black with the blue from step ⑦ to paint the sixth mountain ridge from the back.

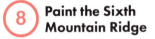

Colors Used: ⑦ Blue + Black

⑨ Paint the Seventh Mountain Ridge

As in step ⑧, mix more black with the blue from step ⑦ to paint the frontmost mountain ridge.

Colors Used: ⑦ Blue + Black

Paint the Trees

⑩ Paint the Trees in the Foreground

Fill in the trees in the foreground with black to complete the painting.

Color Used: Black

Let's Make Colorful Art! **91**

Difficulty Level

How to Paint the Sea

When painting the sea in the summertime, you can create separation between the sky and the sea—even if they are painted with the same blue—by adding clouds between them. For the sandy beach, paint the wet shoreline darker to achieve a beautiful composition.

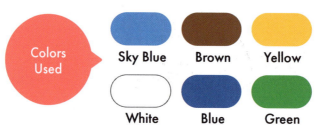

Colors Used: Sky Blue, Brown, Yellow, White, Blue, Green

Sketch the Outlines

Draw the Sky and Sea

Use a pencil to sketch the sky and sea. Also, decide the position of the clouds and the reflections on the surface of the sea.

Paint the Sky and Sea

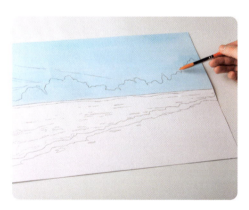

 Paint the Sky

Use diluted sky blue to paint the entire area of the sky, including the clouds.

Color Used   Sky Blue

Paint the Sandy Beach

Mix brown, yellow and white, and then dilute with water to paint the sandy beach.

Colors Used 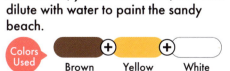 Brown Yellow White

Let's Make Colorful Art! 93

> It's best not to use too much paint—paint with a slightly dry brush.

4 Layer Blue on the Sky

Dilute blue with water, and then wipe the brush lightly with a cloth after loading it up. Lightly brush blue onto the sky.

Color Used — Blue

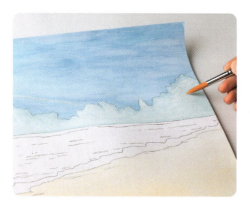

5 Paint the Clouds

Mix sky blue and white, dilute with water, and paint the clouds.

Colors Used — Sky Blue + White

6 Paint the Sea (Part 1)

Dilute blue with water and paint the sea. Trace the horizon line with a darker blue.

Color Used — Blue

7. Paint the Sea (Part 2)

Mix green and blue, dilute with water, and layer it on the sea, avoiding the horizon line from step ⑥.

 Colors Used  Green + Blue

8. Layer the Sandy Beach

Mix brown and yellow, and then dilute with water. Paint the area near the waves darker.

 Colors Used  Brown + Yellow

> Layer the paint to cover the sketch lines!

9. Paint the Highlighted Areas

Dilute white with a small amount of water and paint the highlighted areas of the sea to complete the painting.

Color Used White

Let's Make Colorful Art! 95

Difficulty Level

How to Draw Fireworks

When you want to draw fireworks exploding in the night sky, it is recommended to use crayons, which can create vibrant colors. By layering colors and adjusting their appearance, you can capture the look of the light and smoke of the fireworks in your drawing.

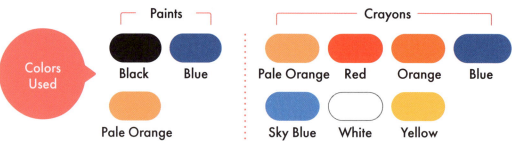

Sketch the Outlines

1
Draw the Fireworks and Smoke

Use a pencil to draw the outlines of the fireworks and smoke.

Paint the Sky and Draw the Fireworks

2 Fill in the Sky

Dilute black with water and paint the sky, covering all the lines of the fireworks.

3 Draw the Smoke

Use a pale orange crayon to color the lower part of the smoke.

Let's Make Colorful Art!

The soft-edged look of the crayon makes the smoke look realistic!

④ Draw the Smoke

Using red, orange and blue crayons, color the smoke with circular motions.

⑤ Draw the Fireworks

Using a sky blue crayon, draw the fireworks, combining long and short strokes.

The color underneath should be slightly visible!

⑥ Add More Smoke

Use the orange crayon to add more smoke.

⑦ Layer with White

Similarly to step ⑤, use a yellow crayon to draw the fireworks. Then, layer with the white crayon over the fireworks and smoke.

8) Layer the Fireworks (Part 1)

Using the blue crayon, trace over the sky blue fireworks from step ⑤.

Color Used: Blue

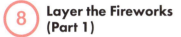

9) Layer the Fireworks (Part 2)

Just like in step ⑧, trace over the yellow fireworks from step ⑦ with the orange crayon.

Color Used: Orange

10) Darken the Sky

Use diluted black paint to further darken the sky.

Color Used: Black

NOTE

It looks beautiful when you lightly paint near the smoke with the same color paint as the smoke.

Let's Make Colorful Art!

Difficulty Level

How to Paint a Rabbit

When you want to show the fluffy fur of an animal, it's good to paint short overlapping strokes. Use a pencil to darken the edges of the rabbit's eye, giving it a glossy look.

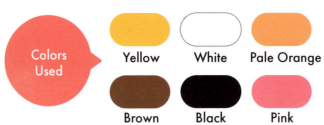

Sketch the Outline

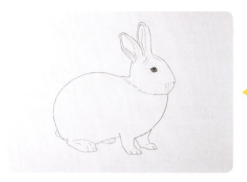

1. Draw the Rabbit

Using a pencil, combine long curves and short, side-by-side lines to draw the rabbit. Add shading to the eyes as well.

NOTE
For the eyes, if you color the outline darker and the inside slightly lighter, they will look 3-D.

Paint the Rabbit

Move the brush to follow the flow of the rabbit's fur!

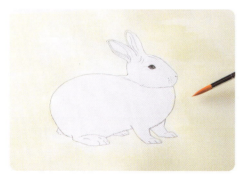

2. Paint the Background

Mix yellow and white with plenty of water to make a thin wash, and then paint the background.

 Colors Used  Yellow + White

3. Paint the Entire Coat

Thin pale orange with water, and then paint the entire rabbit.

 Color Used Pale Orange

Let's Make Colorful Art!

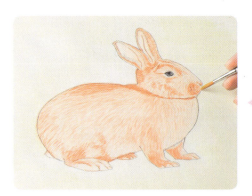

④ Paint the Fur (Part 1)

Mix brown, yellow, and a bit of white with water, and then paint the details of the rabbit's fur. Paint shadows and denser fur parts more heavily.

TIP

When painting fur, imagine the direction in which the rabbit's fur grows and paint accordingly.

Colors Used:  Brown Yellow White

⑤ Paint the Fur (Part 2)

Mix brown, yellow, and a bit of black with water. Paint more fur to cover the entire rabbit.

Colors Used:  Brown Yellow Black

⑥ Paint the Ears and Fur

Dilute pink with water and paint the inside of the nearest ear. Then, add another layer of fur color using the brown from step 5.

Colors Used:  Pink   Brown

Chapter 4

> Fill in the inside of the eyes with the same color.

7 Paint the Fur (Part 3)

Add white to the brown from step 5 and paint the finer fur details.

Colors Used: 5 Brown + White

8 Add Shadows

Mix brown and black with water, and then add shadows to the darker areas.

Colors Used: Brown + Black

9 Paint the Fur on the Face

Using diluted white, paint the fur around the eyes and mouth. Blend it with the brown fur.

Color Used: White

10 Paint the Fur on the Belly

Similar to step 9, use diluted white to paint the fur on the belly, blending it with the brown fur to finish.

Color Used: 9 White

Let's Make Colorful Art! 103

Difficulty Level

How to Paint a Landscape

Let's challenge ourselves with a landscape painting of a complex structure surrounded by trees. The key point is to use colorful hues like those that give a fairy-tale appearance. Adjust the amount of water added to increase and decrease the color saturation for variety.

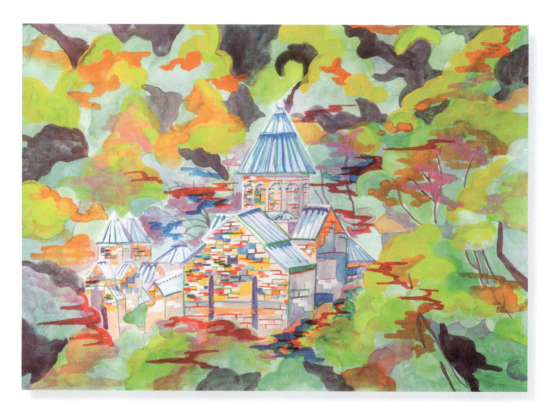

Sketch the Outlines

From the foreground to the background, draw the overlapping trees, walls and roofs.

1 Draw the Structure and Trees

Use a pencil to sketch the structure and trees. Draw the structure first, then add the surrounding trees.

Paint the Trees and Buildings

2 Paint the Trees

Use diluted green to color the trees.

Color Used — Green

3 Paint the Structure

Mix pale orange and white, dilute it with the same amount of water as in step 2, and then color the structure.

Colors Used — Pale Orange + White

Let's Make Colorful Art!

Remember that the light source is in the upper left while adding shadows!

4 Paint the Roofs

Mix sky blue and white, dilute with water to the same consistency as steps 2 and 3, and then color the roofs of the structure.

Sky Blue   White

5 Add Shadows to the Structure

Mix red, blue and white to create a light purple, and use it to color the shadowed areas of the structure.

Red   Blue   White

6 Add Light and Shadows to the Trees

Use yellow-green to color the parts of the trees that are directly sunlit. Add green to the shaded areas.

Yellow-Green   Green

7 Add Darker Shadows

Mix red and blue, dilute with water to create a light purple, and then add shadows to the trees.

Red   Blue

106 Chapter 4

> Changing the amount of water to achieve different intensities will make the painting more beautiful.

8. Paint the Roof Ridges

Using less water than in step 7 to make a more concentrated purple, add ridges to the roofs.

Colors Used: Red + Blue

9. Add Patterns (Part 1)

Using orange and blue, add a brick pattern to the walls.

Colors Used: Orange, Blue

10. Add Patterns (Part 2)

Just like in step 9, add a brick pattern on the walls using white.

Color Used: White

11. Paint Branches

Imagining branches visible through the gaps in the trees, paint the branches with brown.

Color Used: Brown

Let's Make Colorful Art!

12. Add Shadows

Mix red and green to create a color close to black, and then add shadows to the trees.

Colors Used: Red + Green

13. Add Highlights (Part 1)

Use yellow to further brighten the parts of the structure and trees that are sunlit.

Color Used: Yellow

14. Add Highlights (Part 2)

Similarly to step 13, use orange to add warmth to the sunlit parts.

Color Used: Orange

15. Paint Mortar Lines

Dilute green with water and outline the bricks.

Color Used: Green
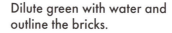

16 Add Pink

Add pink, diluted with water, to the shadows of the bricks and trees.

Pink

17 Trace with Blue

Trace the outlines of the structure with blue diluted with water. Also, add blue around the building.

Blue

Enjoy layering colors as you like.

18 Add Red

Add red to the brick outlines and the shadows around the trees to complete the painting.

Red

Let's Make Colorful Art! 109

Difficulty Level

How to Paint a Car

Painting a shiny car body can be difficult. Refer to the light and shadow discussion (pages 62–63) and study the car carefully to understand the shading. Once you can do this, you'll be great at coloring with paint!

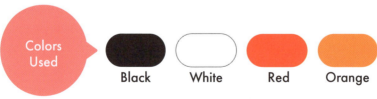

Colors Used: Black, White, Red, Orange

Sketch the Outlines

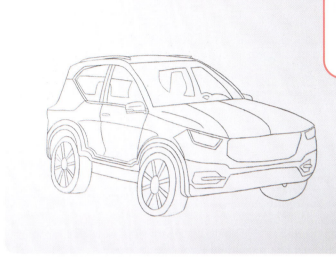

For the interior of the car, just outline the seats without adding too much detail.

① Draw the Car

Use a pencil to draw the car. Also, draw border lines for areas of light and shadow.

Paint the Car

② Paint the Background

Mix black and white, dilute with water, and then paint the background.

Colors Used: Black + White

③ Paint the Car Body (Part 1)

Mix red and orange, dilute with water, and then paint the car body.

Colors Used: Red + Orange

Let's Make Colorful Art!

Softly blur the edges of the shadows for a natural look.

4 Paint the Car Body (Part 2)

Avoiding the red areas painted in step 3, use diluted black to paint the rest of the body and the tires, leaving accents on the wheels and lights untouched.

Color Used: Black

5 Paint Shadows on the Car Body

Dilute black with water and paint the shadows on the car body.

Color Used: Black

6 Paint the Wheels

Mix black and white, dilute with water, and add a pattern of short strokes for the grille. Paint the wheels too.

Colors Used: Black + White

7 Add Details to the Front of the Car

Use the same gray as in step 6 to add fine details to the front parts of the car.

Color Used: 6 Gray

Chapter 4

8. Paint the Highlights

Paint the highlights of the shiny parts of the hood with white.

White

9. Paint Sparkles with Lines

Paint cross-shaped lines with white on the shiny parts. Also, paint the shiny parts of the car body as in step 8.

Color Used — White

10. Paint the Windows

Dilute white with water and paint the windows.

White

11. Add Detail to the Tires

Use diluted black to add details to the wheels. Complete the tires using the same gray as in step 6.

Colors Used — Black — Gray (6)

Let's Make Colorful Art! **113**

TRY IT RIGHT AWAY!

Using Colored Pencils

Colored pencils, which are easy to use, are recommended for anyone who struggles with coloring.

Difficulty Level

Basic Coloring Technique

This basic coloring technique can be used not only when coloring your own drawings but also when coloring in coloring books. Make sure you don't oversharpen the colored pencils.

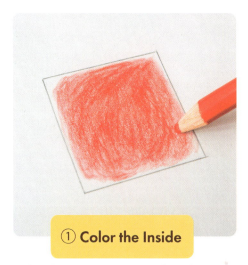

① Color the Inside

Color the entire area, avoiding the very edges. Because layering the colors will make unevenness less noticeable, don't worry about consistency at first.

② Color the Edges

Once you've colored the inside, color up to the edges. If you have trouble coloring right up to the edges, you can slightly sharpen the pencil tip for this step.

Tips for Coloring Well

As with paint, focus on layering light colors to gradually darken them. Additionally, by layering different colors, you can blend colors even with colored pencils.

Layer light colors to darken them

If you color too darkly at first, you might leave pencil marks and be unable to blend colors. Start gently and lightly.

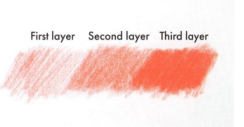

First layer   Second layer   Third layer

Blending colors with layering

Just as with paint, start with the lightest or most transparent color when using two (or three) colors. If you start with a dark color, you won't be able to layer it.

The type of paper changes the drawing

The appearance of colors changes depending on the paper surface. Kent paper is less prone to unevenness, while drawing paper gives a warm, textured look.

Kent paper

Drawing paper

Let's Make Colorful Art!

Difficulty Level

How to Draw Flowers

[Colored Pencils]

Drawings made with colored pencils look soft compared to artwork painted with watercolors. Refer to the coloring techniques on pages 114–115.

• The underlying sketch is the same as the one used on page 74.

Colors Used — Colored Pencils

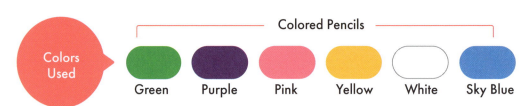

Green   Purple   Pink   Yellow   White   Sky Blue

Chapter 4

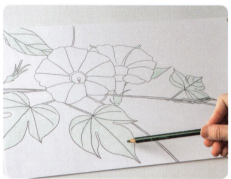

① Color the Leaves

Lightly color the leaves, vines and buds with green.

Green

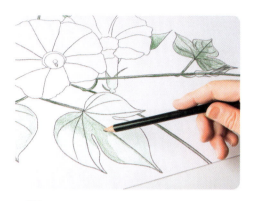

② Add Shadows to the Leaves

Layer green to add shadows and darken certain parts of the leaves.

 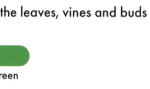
Green

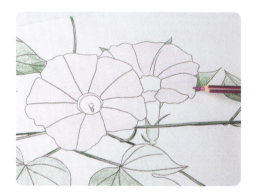

③ Color the Petals

Lightly color the petals entirely with purple.

Purple

④ Add Shadows to the Petals

Layer purple to add shadows and darken certain parts of the petals.

Purple

Let's Make Colorful Art!

5 | Layer the Petals

Layer pink over the entire area of the petals.

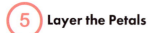
Color Used — Pink

6 | Color the Brightly Lit Parts

Add yellow to the parts of the flowers, leaves, vines and buds that catch the light.

Color Used — Yellow

7 | Layer the Shadows

In contrast to step 6, add purple to the shadowed parts of the flowers, leaves, vines and buds.

Color Used — Purple

8 | Layer the Leaves

Darken the leaves, vines and buds by layering on green.

Color Used — Green

9 — Add Shadows to the Center of the Flower

Shade the center of the flower with green.

Color Used: Green

10 — Darken the Petals

Just like in step 5, further darken the petals with pink.

Color Used: Pink

11 — Add Highlights

Use white to emphasize the bright parts of the petals and blend with other colors.

Color Used: White

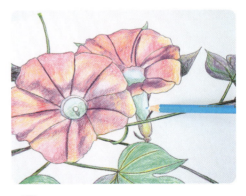

12 — Layer the Center of the Flower

Layer sky blue on the center of the flower.

Color Used: Sky Blue

Let's Make Colorful Art!

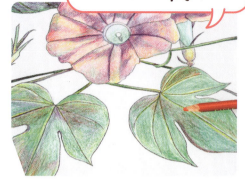

> Use the method of mixing complementary colors to create muddy shadows (see page 58).

⑬ Layer the Shadows on the Petals

Further layer green over the shadows on the petals.

Color Used — Green

⑭ Layer the Shadows on the Leaves

Layer red over the shadows on the leaves.

Color Used — Red

⑮ Draw the Patterns on the Petals

Color Used — Pink

Add patterns to the flowers to complete the drawing.

Colored Pencil Example

Flowers

A piece combining the best aspects of colored pencils and watercolor paints.

Coloring large areas with colored pencils can be tiresome, so it's good to cover the entire area with paint, and then use colored pencils for shading.

This piece intentionally takes advantage of the colored pencil lines to capture the look of the fabric's texture.

Let's Make Colorful Art!

Appendix A

Color Blends

Mixing Primary Colors

Red + Blue → Purple

Red Red + Blue → Reddish Purple

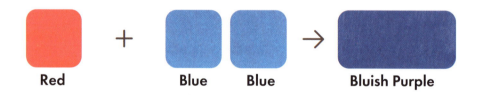

Red + Blue Blue → Bluish Purple

Red + Yellow → Orange

Red + Yellow Yellow → Yellowish Orange

Practice using the chart so you can create the colors you want!

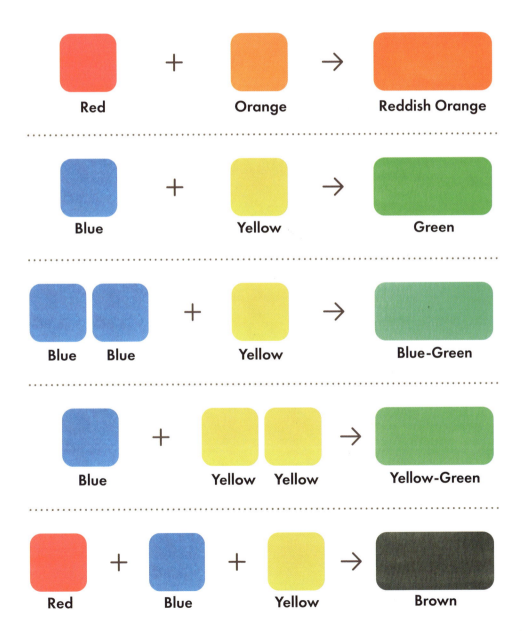

Appendix B

Color Mixing Charts

Mixing with White

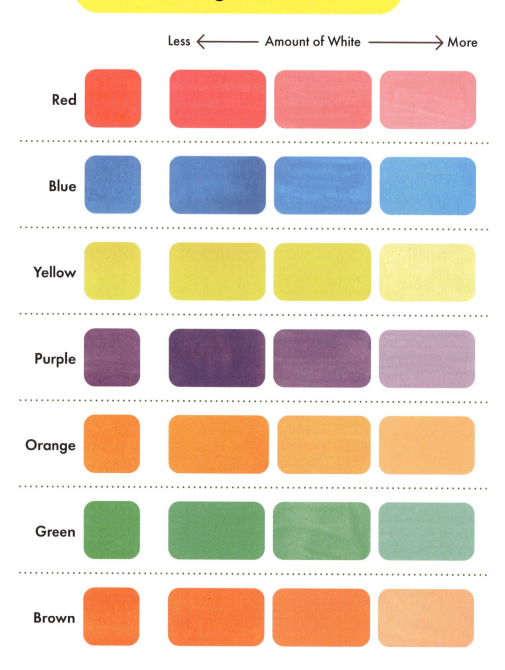

Mixing with Black

Conclusion

Drawing is truly a creative activity. The drawings you create as a youngster can only be drawn at that specific stage in your life. If you draw a lot, you'll grow and improve more and more. Even if you can't see it yourself, comparing your previous drawings with the new ones will make the progress clear and will surely surprise you.

That's why I want you to draw as many pictures as you can right now. And I hope that the artwork you create will become lifelong treasures.

You've probably noticed that AI (artificial intelligence) has evolved to the point where it can create realistic images. AI art is very polished, but it will never be the same as drawings and paintings made by human hands.

Afterword

It will take a significant amount of practice before you can fully capture the charm of painting and drawing with color.

Painting and drawing are meaningful activities, so I encourage you to practice a lot while using this book as a guide. If you find an object or a scene you want to recreate beyond the subjects that are introduced in this book, keep expressing yourself freely with your own colors and methods.

I hope that this book will be helpful to you as you progress in your creative journey. Finally, I would like to express my heartfelt gratitude to everyone involved in the production of this book.

．．

—Koichi Matsuda
Director of Azabu Atelier

"Books to Span the East and West"

Tuttle Publishing was founded in 1832 in the small New England town of Rutland, Vermont [USA]. Our core values remain as strong today as they were then—to publish best-in-class books which bring people together one page at a time. In 1948, we established a publishing outpost in Japan—and Tuttle is now a leader in publishing English-language books about the arts, languages and cultures of Asia. The world has become a much smaller place today and Asia's economic and cultural influence has grown. Yet the need for meaningful dialogue and information about this diverse region has never been greater. Over the past seven decades, Tuttle has published thousands of books on subjects ranging from martial arts and paper crafts to language learning and literature—and our talented authors, illustrators, designers and photographers have won many prestigious awards. We welcome you to explore the wealth of information available on Asia at www.tuttlepublishing.com.

Published by Tuttle Publishing, an imprint of Periplus Editions (HK) Ltd.

www.tuttlepublishing.com

ISBN 978-0-8048-5831-1

Shogakusei no Tame no E ga Gunto Jozu ni Naru
Iro no Tsukaikata Nurikata Lesson
Copyright © FIGINC 2023
English translation rights arranged with
MATES universal contents Co., Ltd.
through Japan UNI Agency, Inc., Tokyo

English translation © 2025 Periplus Editions (HK) Ltd

All rights reserved. The items (text, photographs, drawings, etc.) included in this book are solely for personal use, and may not be reproduced for commercial purposes without permission of the copyright holders.

Printed in Malaysia   2501VP

28 27 26 25
10 9 8 7 6 5 4 3 2 1

Distributed by:

North America, Latin America & Europe
Tuttle Publishing
364 Innovation Drive
North Clarendon
VT 05759-9436 U.S.A.
Tel: (802) 773-8930
Fax: (802) 773-6993
info@tuttlepublishing.com
www.tuttlepublishing.com

Asia Pacific
Berkeley Books Pte. Ltd.
3 Kallang Sector, #04-01
Singapore 349278
Tel: (65) 6741-2178
Fax: (65) 6741-2179
inquiries@periplus.com.sg
www.tuttlepublishing.com

TUTTLE PUBLISHING® is a registered trademark of Tuttle Publishing, a division of Periplus Editions (HK) Ltd.